The Manx Grand Prix

Murray McLeod

Copyright © Murray McLeod 2015

All rights reserved.

This book is copyright protected. Apart from any fair dealings for the purpose of private study, criticism, research or review as permitted under the *Copyright Act (Australia)*, no part may be reproduced by any process without written permission from the copyright owner.

ISBN-13: 978-1511745482
ISBN-10: 1511745487

Sports/Motor sport history

This book, and others by Murray McLeod may be purchased on www.amazon.com online bookstores and other retailers.

The author has taken all possible care to give appropriate acknowledgement and seek permissions from all interested parties and welcomes any further correspondence. Enquiries should be addressed to the copyright owner.

Interior design and cover creation: Linda Ruth Brooks

PHOTOGRAPHIC ACKNOWLEDGMENTS
Photo reference and race results;
The Motor Cycle
Francis Beart (Jeff Clew 1978)
Isle of Man TT (Deane 1975)
Rider portraits; The author

DEDICATION

To riders, novice or veteran
leather clad and helmeted
they dared to challenge
the odds

Contents

A review of three decades of a famous road race series 5

A selection of Manx Winners 1927-1952 23

    Tim Hunt 24

    Doug Pirie 28

    Austin Munks 32

    Freddie Frith 36

    Harold Daniell 40

    John White 46

    Maurice Cann 52

    Dennis Parkinson 58

    Kenneth Bills 64

    Ernie Lyons 70

    Eric Briggs 78

    Cromie McCandless 82

    Geoff Duke 88

    David Bennett 94

    Bob McIntyre 100

Author's Tribute 110

Author profile 112

The Manx Grand Prix

A review of three decades of a famous road race series

(1923-1953)

International motorcycle racing owes an eternal debt to the Isle of Man Parliament with its attitude to road racing, which apart from its spectacle became an incentive to tourism.

In a world where Formula One and Moto GP events are fought out on custom-built circuits, the Isle of Man is one of the few venues where public roads are closed for motorcycle racing and practicing.

This state of affairs had its origins as far back as 1907 with the inaugural Tourist Trophy races.

The title 'Tourist Trophy' is significant, for the competitors were entered on touring machines, similar to those sold to the public, rather than specialized track racers.

Two categories were available in the actual race; one for single-cylinder machines and one for those of twin-cylinder configuration, but in different race classes.

No engine or weight limits were imposed; however a strict fuel ration of 75 miles per gallon for the twins and 90 miles per gallon for the singles was in force, thus ensuring that any oversized racing engines would be ineligible.

The course chosen for this Homeric 1907 event and for the ensuing four years was the abbreviated St. John's circuit, 15.8 miles in length and situated to the west of the Island.

With roads little more than hard-packed mud, strewn with flint and rocks and heavily rutted with horse-drawn traffic, these were testing times for the aspiring road racers.

Their machines too were basic in the extreme; of side-valve design with single speeds, belt drive and total-loss lubrication, they were still hard-pressed to surmount anything but the mildest of gradients, even with the pedal assistance then permitted.

Twenty five hardy souls faced the starter for that epic 158 miles event, and not surprisingly the attrition rate was fairly high.

The MANX Grand Prix

St John's Circuit

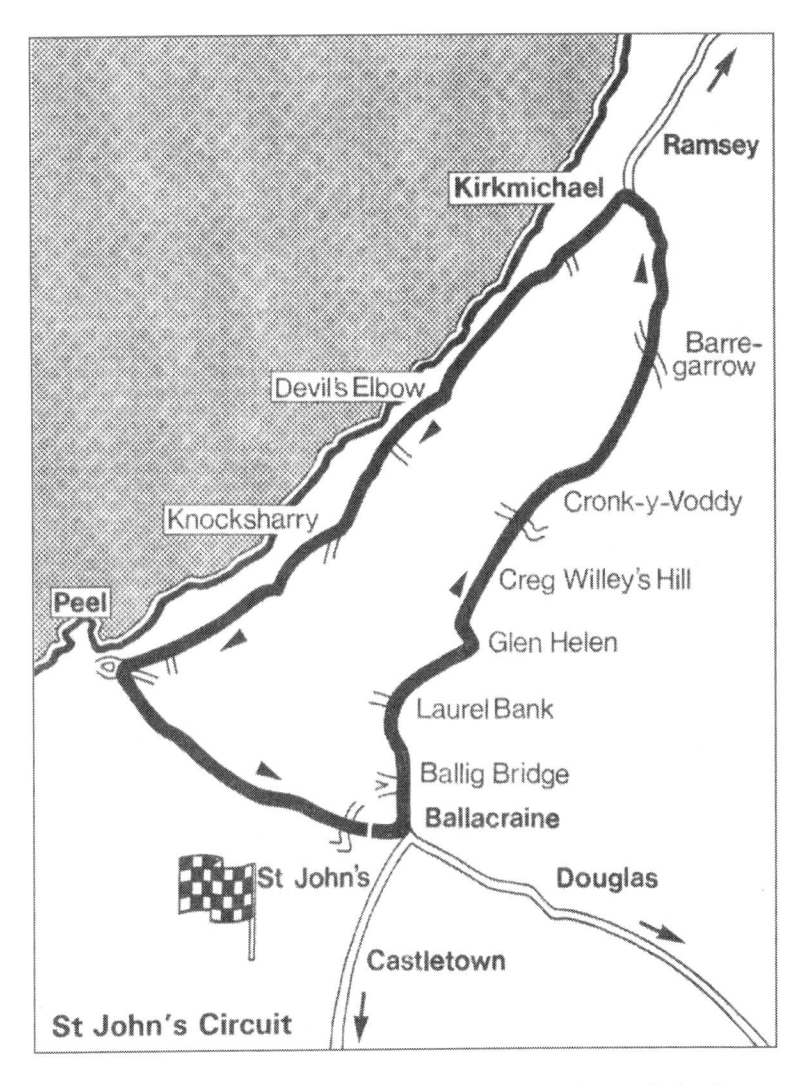

Fifteen machines succumbed to the diabolic conditions and at the finish two makes put their name to a prestigious trophy.

Charles Collier on a Matchless won the single-cylinder class at an average speed of 38.22 mph, while in the twin-cylinder category Rem Fowler brought his Norton home at a respectable 36.22 mph. and also recorded the fastest lap at 42.9 mph.

In that four-year span of the St. John's circuit, the Collier brothers, Charlie and Harry made quite an impact, registering three wins in that period, thus adding prestige to their 'Matchless' brand of motor cycles.

James Norton followed a similar path with the machines that bore his name; to the extent that every year from 1907 to the mid-1970's Norton were represented at the TT.

In 1911 the TT was transferred to the 37 mile Mountain circuit, long regarded as the most challenging in the world. In the interim, significant improvements had been made to the current machines, which were opportune; as the challenge of the Mountain would have been an almost insurmountable barrier to those 1907 veterans.

Two classes were introduced for the 1911 event; a Senior category for 500cc machines and a Junior for 350's. The transatlantic Senior challenge transposed into the first three places being occupied by Indian machines; while in the Junior, P.J. Evans on a Humber took first place, ahead of the persistent Harry Collier on a Matchless.

In the period 1912-1914 British bikes generally dominated both classes, with Indian machines claiming minor places in 1913 and 1914.

Rudge, Triumph, AJS, Scott and Douglas were firms that featured in those results and would continue supporting the TT in the post-war period and into the 1930's, while more obscure makes like Forward, Vindec and Ivy Green would eventually succumb to falling demand.

A handful of pre-war riders also featured in the post-war period and deserve mention as TT winners; Eric Williams, 1914 and 1921 Junior TT winner with AJS and Cyril Williams (no relation), second in the 1914 Junior and first in the 1920 Junior, also with AJS.

Howard Davies, at age 18 was second in the 1914 Senior on a work's Sunbeam and remarkably first in the 1921 Senior on a 350 AJS.

Even more memorable was his first place in the 1925 Senior, riding a machine of his own manufacture, the HRD.

The extroverted and innovative engineer Freddie Dixon made an unsuccessful appearance at the 1912 Senior TT on a Cleveland, while post-war he had three Senior TT leader board finishes.

Mountain Circuit

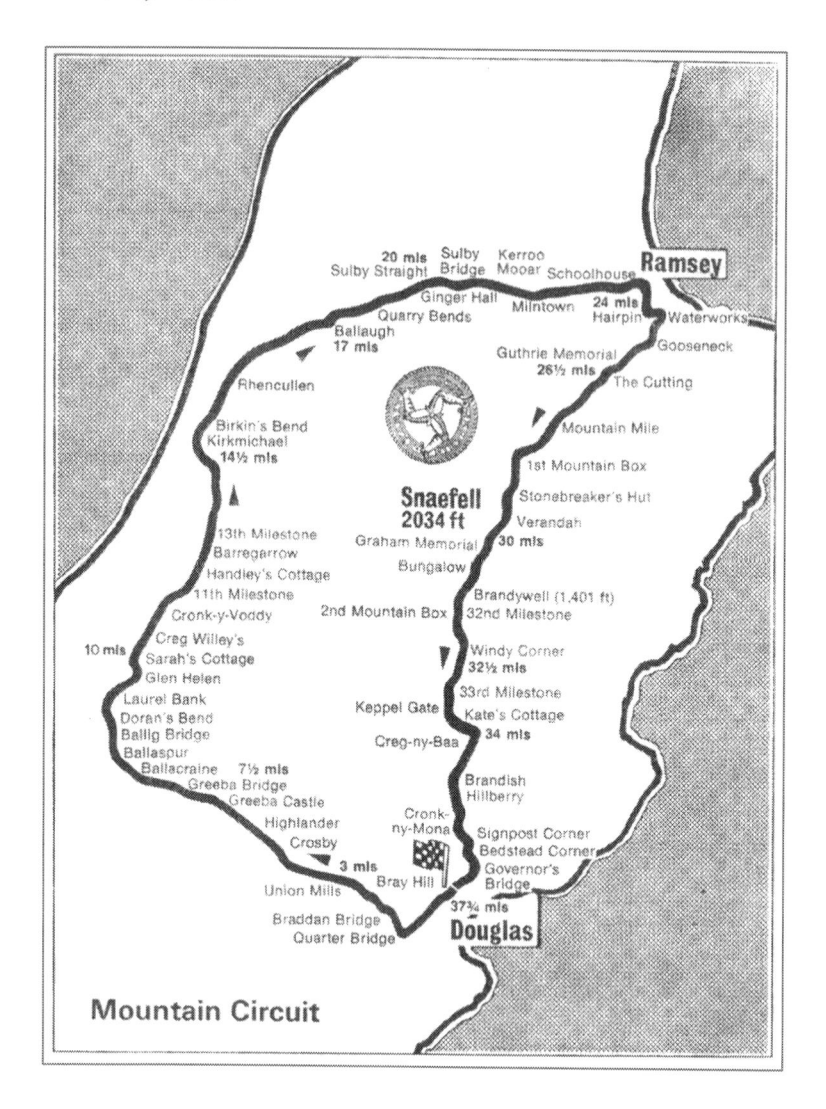

In 1923 he scored a decisive win for Douglas in the inaugural Sidecar TT, while in 1927, to demonstrate his versatility he won the Junior TT on an HRD.

With the end of hostilities in 1918 the racing community was understandably looking forward to a resumption of racing, in particular at the Isle of Man. The TT in fact was revived in 1920, and an interesting inclusion was a 250cc Junior class to supplement the regular 500 Senior and 350 Junior categories.

The 250 race was a bonanza for Levis machines with a 1-2-3 result; while in 1922 the racer/journalist Geoff Davison scored another win for Levis, which proved to be the firm's last Island victory.

The 1920 TT series would appear to have been a success; however two factors were emerging to create an air of insecurity about the TT's future. Already, the amateur riders, who had little chance against the work's sponsored professionals, were lobbying for a better deal; to the extent of creating a series barring non-amateurs.

The proponents of the scheme were a group of young Manx residents, all of them members of the Manx Motor Cycle Club; a group of amateurs whose appeals were noted by the Auto Cycle Union, organizers of the TT events.

The other unsettling factor was an invitation from Belgium to hold the 1921 TT series in that country. Fortunately the Belgian appeal was eventually rejected by the ACU; had those events gone abroad the loss to the Isle of Man would have bordered on disastrous.

With the TT situation stabilized, plans were being formulated for the new Amateur series and with ACU consent they were accorded the lengthy title of 'The Manx Amateur Motor Cycle Race'. Thankfully this was presently shortened to 'Amateur TT; however the contentious issue was the definition of 'Amateur'.

In a sport where amateurs and professionals frequently competed against one another, the question arose; which riders belonged to the former and which to the latter?

In essence it was defined as one who did not accept bonuses from firms supplying motorcycle accessories. This was extended to exclude anybody (including dealers) in the motorcycle business, plus anyone who permitted himself to be used for advertising purposes.

Another issue, which was a feature of the TT, was the exclusion of bookmakers; on the course, in the club enclosure or in the paddock.

While not ideal the system was the best that was available at the time, and by the summer of 1923 the stage was set for the inaugural Amateur TT. In its favour were the excellent facilities enjoyed by the TT; the splendid circuit and grandstands, plus the ample pits and paddock.

Two trophies were donated; to be presented to the winning riders; one from an ex-mayor of Douglas for the Senior winner and one from the proprietors of 'The Motor Cycle' magazine to be presented to the winning Junior.

September 30 1923 saw the launch of an historic series; albeit with a rather small entry of 33 riders facing the starter; 29 on 500cc machines and the rest on 350's.

All machines were competing simultaneously over a prescribed five laps and despite utterings from the pessimists that they would not complete one lap; no less than half the field completed the course.

Winner of the 500cc class was Len Randles on a Sunbeam at a speed of 52.77 mph, while in the Junior Ken Twemlow on a New Imperial finished only fractionally slower at 52.46 mph.

The following year Ken Twemlow moved to the TT, where he won the Junior, again on a New Imperial at a speed of 56.67 mph, and to reinforce the family connection his brother Edwin won the 250

Lightweight; a feat he would repeat at the 1925 TT.

All things considered the 1923 Amateur event was deemed a success; however the practice period was marred with an accident at Hillberry involving Ned Brew, who later succumbed to his injuries. This unfortunate incident highlighted the sheer vastness of the Mountain circuit in coping with accidents.

What the course needed was travelling marshals to handle such mishaps. Eventually this became a reality although not until the 1935 TT series, with Vic Brittain and Arthur Simcock installed in those roles.

'Digger' Simcock was an Aussie ex-pat who competed at the TT from 1931 to 1933 and eventually settled in the UK. Vic Brittain was one of the sport's superb all-rounders and rode in the TT on a regular basis from 1930 to 1934.

The 1923 race was considered to have had a successful outcome, and as the event proceeded into the mid-1920's, two distinctly different types of riders began to emerge.

Firstly were the dedicated ones, generally more skilful than their contemporaries and keen to advance their careers to an international level, generally via the TT. On the other hand were those content to make an impression, but without a commitment to venture into the professional world that lay beyond.

A prime example of the former were the Twemlow brothers, when after a good showing in the 1923 Amateur they both had winning rides at the 1924 TT series.

One needs to remember that in those days the TT was still open to the amateur as well as the professional, provided that the former resisted the temptation to accept bonuses from manufacturers.

The 1924 Amateur TT was another Senior victory for Randles; while in the Junior R.C. Brown emerged as the winner, both Sunbeam mounted. Another rider who attracted favourable comment was C.J.P. Dodson who finished in ninth place on a 350 Sunbeam, while on the same machine Dodson's 1925 TT debut resulted in eighth.

Charlie went on to achieve TT greatness with a Senior win in 1928, followed by a second Senior in 1929, all on Sunbeams.

A significant feature of the 1925 event was the non-restriction on the type of machine entered; where previously entries had been confined to standard stock models. This was also the final year of the prescribed five laps for entrants, and for 1926 and beyond this was increased to six laps, with a total distance of 226½ miles for Seniors and Juniors.

Norton machines were well to the fore in the Senior event, with a 1-2-3 finish for Norton riders, although manufacturers were barred from advertising race results in the interest of maintaining the amateur status of the series.

Interest in the TT appeared to be waning, while the Amateur TT was becoming increasingly popular, with entries almost doubling those of the inaugural 1923 event.

New names were emerging also; riders who would gain renown on the international scene, with Percy Hunt a Senior winner in 1927 and 1928. 'Tim' Hunt, as he was universally named became a stalwart of the official Norton team from 1931 to 1933; and in 1931 became the first rider to score a Senior/Junior TT double.

Tim's celebrated career finished badly at the 1933 Swedish Grand Prix, following a horrendous race crash. He never raced again and is remembered as one of the greatest of his decade.

Another noted rider was Ted Mellors, whose 1927

Amateur foray on a P & M resulted in 10th place. During the 1930's Ted was an active member of the Continental Circus, initially on New Imperials. His fortunes improved markedly in 1936 with his move to Velocette, culminating in 1938 when he became 350 European Champion; plus a Lightweight victory on a Benelli at the 1939 TT.

Meanwhile the Amateur races were subject to further development, when in 1928 Tuesdays and Thursdays were adopted as race days; with the Junior class being run as a separate event. Another addition was a new trophy to be awarded to the Junior race winner; the inaugural recipient being Harry Meaghan on a Rex Acme.

The following year, 1929 proved to be a time of discontent; resulting in the disqualification of the winners of both races.

Previous Junior winner Harry Meaghan was deemed to be the 1929 Junior victor; however a protest was lodged by another rider that Meaghan had received assistance from a spectator, following a roadside halt to repair a damaged throttle cable.

Meaghan protested that he was unaware of the assistance, but the verdict went against him; with E.N. Lea (not the competitor who made the protest) being awarded the trophy.

The dramas were yet unfinished, when Senior race winner D.J. Potts was also excluded. His problems were related to accepting bonuses relating to oil suppliers, and once again Eric Lea, runner-up in both races being awarded the Senior Trophy, thus becoming the first 'amateur' double winner.

In all there were 21 disqualifications during and after the 1929 races; all related to the precise definition of the word 'amateur'.

This proved to be the last 'Amateur TT' and following discussions between the Auto Cycle Union and the Manx Motor Cycle Club, 1930 saw the birth of the Manx Grand Prix.

The race programme continued unchanged, with Junior and Senior races run over six laps, while a significant inclusion was a 250 Lightweight GP being included in the 1934 program; the race being run concurrently with the six lap Junior.

Manx Grand Prix entries continued to increase during the 1930's; with 101 riders taking part in 1930 and by 1934 the total was an impressive 129.

Already two distinct classes of riders were emerging; on one hand were the keen types, anxious to graduate, (if that was the appropriate term) to the TT and possible work's status. Typical of these were Freddie Frith, John White and Harold Daniell; all of whom became members of the illustrious 1930's Norton team.

On the other hand were the perennial amateurs, remaining loyal to the Manx Grand Prix; Dennis Parkinson and Austin Munks were two outstanding examples; another loyal duo was the Rowell brothers, Harold and Bertie, both pre-war and post-war.

In 1938 Ken Bills scored a decisive double on Nortons prepared by technician Steve Lancefield, and despite rumours of war throughout 1939 the Manx Club made plans to conduct the series for that September. Sadly their prospects were doomed to cancellation following Britain's declaration of war on 3 September.

One aspect of the 1939 series was a substantial amount of spares and engines dispatched to the Island by Norton Motors prior to the cancellation. These were providentially stored there for the duration, and with the resumption of the series in 1946, privileged customers were able to acquire what were essentially brand new Nortons.

With the end of hostilities in 1945, the Manx MCC performed something of a minor miracle in re-staging the series in 1946. Quite a few of the pre-war stalwarts were starters along with a new generation of aspiring hopefuls. With vital components like tyres and spark plugs in short supply this was certainly not the time to be chasing records.

Dark horse for the Senior race was Irishman Ernie Lyons, entered on a prototype Triumph twin, and mindful of the diabolically wet conditions that prevailed during the actual race, Lyons finished first, ahead of the usual swarm of Nortons, headed by Ken Bills, securing a hardy second place.

Better conditions were a feature of the 1947 series, with Eric Briggs securing a memorable double.

Following Ernie Lyons' 1946 win, Triumph rather tardily marketed replicas of his machine, named the Triumph Grand Prix, and on one of these, Don Crossley scored a handy win in the 1948 Senior ahead of a phalanx of Nortons.

Geoff Duke and Cromie McCandless were two riders who dominated the 1949 series; with McCandless taking the Junior and Duke the Senior.

By 1951 the series had entered the Norton 'Featherbed' era, and thus equipped Dave Bennett recorded the first Senior win for the new model.

The following year saw a new contestant in the

Senior class, the prototype Matchless G45, on which Derek Farrant scored an inaugural win, and in the process raised the lap record to 89.64 mph.

1952 held painful memories for Francis Beart with his nomination of Ivor Arber as his rider. RAF member, Arber had been awarded a decoration for a meritorious act during his RAF tenure and was also a TT winner; in this instance, the 1951 Senior Clubman's at the Isle of Man.

No doubt the Beart/Arber duo was quietly confident of a good showing at the 1952 Manx; however tragedy struck during an early practice session. It was reported that Arber failed to negotiate Hillberry; simply going straight ahead and hitting the bank at high speed on his Senior Norton.

With the rider killed and the machine a write-off, Beart was preparing to return to the mainland when he was approached by retired world champion Bob Foster with the proposal that his rider Ken James take over Arber's Junior entry. Rather unwillingly Beart agreed; and then on James' third practice lap he crashed fatally at Cronk-ny-Mona.

With two riders killed and both machines written off this was a tragic outcome for all concerned.

In 1953, and on the eve of his retirement from racing, Manx veteran Dennis Parkinson had the satisfaction of achieving that elusive Senior victory.

Here was a race that went down to the wire, with Parkinson edging out Norton-mounted Bob Keeler and local rider Derek Ennett on a G45 Matchless.

This concludes our coverage of the first thirty years of a famous race series, which survived those somewhat ambiguous events of the 1920's to emerge as arguably the greatest and best supported road races of all time.

The following pages feature a selection of profiles of winners from those formative years together with pencil portraits by the author.

A selection of Manx Winners

1927-1952

Tim Hunt

Doug Pirie

Austin Munks

Freddie Frith

Harold Daniell

John White

Maurice Cann

Dennis Parkinson

Kenneth Bills

Ernie Lyons

Eric Briggs

Cromie McCandless

Geoff Duke

David Bennett

Bob McIntyre

Murray McLeod

Tim Hunt

Tim Hunt burst on the racing scene in the style of a shooting star. His star burned brightly for a few seasons and then abruptly it was extinguished. He was born in Manchester in 1908 and christened Percy but from an early age he was labeled 'Tim' after a comic book character named 'Tiger Tim'. Apart from his riding ability he was also blessed with wealthy parents, to the extent that Mrs. Hunt was quite happy to provide the funds to launch Tim on his chosen career.

His first road racing success was the Senior class of the 1927 Amateur TT. Mounted on a new CS1 Norton he won again in 1928 and in the process he broke Stanley Woods' Senior TT lap record. These efforts did not go unnoticed by Norton talent scouts and Tim was eagerly signed up as a Norton teamster. A measure of Hunt's versatility and also the CS1 Norton's was demonstrated when he rode his race bike in the 1928 Scottish Six Day's Trial and collected a first class award in that strenuous event.

Despite a lack of engine skills it was rare for him to suffer mechanical failures; his great ability was in his natural riding talents. In 1931 he became the first rider to score a Junior/Senior double at the TT, with fastest lap in the Junior. The Senior was also memorable for teammate Jimmie Simpson who recorded the first-ever 80mph lap. Not surprisingly he failed to finish, once again reinforcing his nickname 'Unlucky Jim'.

In the continental races it was Hunt and Woods who generally rode the 500s while Guthrie and Simpson handled the 350s. Such was Norton's domination during the era that it was headline news when they occasionally finished out of the money. Of the twelve classic races of 1932 that Norton contested they won eleven. The team for the 1933 season remained unchanged; with Stanley Woods once more the star of the TT series after repeating his 1932 Junior/Senior double. From there the team moved to the continent to contest the classic events; where the spoils were fairly evenly shared between Hunt and Woods in the opening rounds with Hunt having success in the 350 Swiss Grand Prix and 500 class at the Dieppe and Belgian Grands Prix.

Following the Ulster Grand prix, which saw a popular victory for Stanley Woods, the team travelled to Saxtorp to contest the Swedish Grand Prix, which was also that year's European Grand Prix. It proved to be a disaster for Nortons and particularly so for Tim Hunt. Their greatest challenge was expected to come from the Swedish Husqvarna team of Sunnqvist and Kalen. As the race progressed, Woods, Hunt and Sunnqvist were slip-streaming one another down the main straight when a rider they were lapping slowed dramatically. Woods and Sunnqvist both made a miraculous avoidance but Hunt careered into him. When Tim was retrieved by the ambulance team he was found to have suffered a seriously smashed hip, while the other rider, a Norwegian was tragically killed.

This unfortunate incident was a sad ending to Hunt's career. He spent three months in a Swedish hospital before being transferred by plane to England for further surgery. Medical technology was not advanced enough in those days to plate shattered limbs, resulting in Tim spending the next five years in and out of hospital. After many operations he finished up with one leg shorter than the other. He never raced again. Tim's contemporaries were agreed that if he could have been more serious about his attitude to racing he would have been the greatest ever. Tim believed in living life to the full and being serious was just not in his make-up.

Joe Craig held Tim Hunt in the highest regard and years later he confided to his current champion Geoff Duke that of all the riders he was involved with, he regarded just two as having that innate riding excellence ; 'Tim Hunt and Geoff Duke'.

Murray McLeod

Doug Pirie

One of the staunchest supporters of the Manx Grand Prix during the 1930's was Doug Pirie. An architect/surveyor by profession he was also one of the more successful regarding his ratio of wins. A loyal Velocette adherent, his first Manx essay was the 1929 Amateur Road Race, which resulted in a seventh place in the Junior, while his Scott entry earned him fifth in the Senior.

From 1929 to 1934 Pirie was entered in the Junior and Senior categories, and with varying degrees of success or retirement. In only his second essay at the Manx, in 1930 he scored a worthy Junior win on the Velo; while on the same 350 he finished fourth in the Senior. The following year 1931, he claimed another Junior win, again Velocette-mounted. Unusually his Senior bike was an Excelsior, which unfortunately resulted in retirement. In 1932 he rode Excelsiors in both categories, and once again they only provided retirements.

Using Junior and Senior Nortons in 1933, his fortunes improved to the extent of a third in the Junior, while his Senior Norton failed to finish. Still using Nortons in 1934 Pirie's fortunes gained markedly when he finished second in the Junior to Cambridge undergraduate John White, a talented rider who went on to become a regular Norton work's member from 1935 to 1939. The Senior race provided its share of excitement, with White leading until he was delayed by a loose spark plug lead. He restarted, only to retire following a crash at Union Mills. He did at least have the satisfaction of fastest lap at 81.71 mph. Meantime Doug Pirie powered his way to first place ahead of J.K. Swanston, a regular Manx entrant and also a medical practitioner.

Following a successful Manx career Pirie made the decision to transfer to the 1935 TT series, with entries in all categories; Junior, Lightweight and Senior. His Junior mount was a Velocette; with a New Imperial for the Lightweight. Pirie was of quite large build and one wonders how the 250 New Imp would cope with his bulk?

Rather than his usual Norton, Pirie's Senior mount was a Vincent HRD, a bike which had a good reputation for handling and braking, although down on maximum speed compared to the camshaft Norton.

Monday's Junior TT brought a good result for Pirie, gaining fourth place behind the official Norton team, comprising Guthrie, Rusk and White, making Pirie the first private entrant to finish in such exalted company. Wednesday's Lightweight TT got away under unpleasant conditions of rain and mist on parts of the course, especially on the Mountain.

It was under such challenges that Doug Pirie somehow misjudged the 33rd Milestone on his fifth lap and crashed heavily, fatally as it later transpired. His passing was a great loss to the racing fraternity, and it was not unreasonable to suggest that Doug Pirie was poised on the brink of work's status.

The author recalls a photo of Doug Pirie seated on his Vincent HRD, following a 1935 practice session, and rather than his usual personable attitude, his visage displays extreme sadness, causing one to wonder if he held some premonition about the forthcoming races.

A rather poignant gesture was the donation of the present Lightweight GP Trophy, presented to the Manx Motor Cycle Club by the family of Doug Pirie.

Murray McLeod

Austin Munks

Lincolnshire rider Austin Munks, like many of his contemporaries was a Velocette adherent, making his first Manx essay in the 1931 Junior MGP. It began as an outstanding debut for the 22 years old Munks, leading the race from the start until he was forced to retire on his last lap. This was cruel misfortune for the newcomer; however in the 1932 Junior MGP he was compensated somewhat with a steady third place.

Munks was fortunate in having his machines prepared by good friend Sam Coupland; thus creating a formidable duo in their racing partnership, which was demonstrated in 1933 with Munks' emphatic win at the Junior MGP. The following year, 1934 and still on Velocettes he gained another third place in the Junior MGP, in a race won by future Norton teamster, John White.

Around this period Munks lost his left eye in a shooting accident; however with commendable grit he adjusted to the handicap and in 1936 he achieved the first MGP Junior/Senior double, using a Velocette for the Junior and a Norton for the Senior. Munks did not feature in further pre-war race wins; although he made an appearance at the 1947 Lightweight MGP, this time on a Moto Guzzi. An interesting aspect was that three Guzzis were entered in the Lightweight, with pre-war

Lightweight Manx winner Ron Harris and Irish newcomer Benji Russell so-equipped.

Russell was a protégé of the legendary Stanley Woods, who also acted as his entrant. An exciting scrap began, involving Russell, Munks and Freddie Hawken on an Excelsior, with Russell gaining the lead, which he maintained until lap five. Tragedy struck during that lap when approaching Ramsey, Russell struck a manhole cover, crashed and was killed instantly. As a result of this sad mishap Munks inherited the lead, which he held to the finish, thus gaining his fourth MGP win.

On retiring from racing Munks was remembered for sponsoring promising young riders; in fact it was Geoff Duke who approached Austin Munks in 1952 with a view to becoming a Gilera team member; such was the influence and trust that Munks enjoyed with the Italian factories, Duke was welcomed as a Gilera team member; going on to win three world championships for the firm. Two riders who also deserve mention were R.H. (Dickie) Dale and Bernard Codd.

Following a Guzzi win in the 1948 Lightweight Manx, Dale went on to attain 'works' status with a variety of factories; Norton, MV Agusta and importantly Moto Guzzi, with whom he scored notable wins. His death in 1961 at the Nurburgring aroused profound sadness for Sam Coupland and Austin Munks; to the extent of Coupland interring Dale's ashes in his garden.

Bernard Codd's career was notable in scoring a Senior/Junior double at the 1956 Clubman's TT at the Isle of Man. His machines were the ubiquitous BSA DBD Gold Star; yet such was the dominance of the 'Goldie' that it led eventually to the discontinuation of the Clubman series. Production of the 'Goldie' was terminated in 1962 and its passing is still mourned; with surviving examples commanding astronomical prices.

Austin Munks operated a thriving Jaguar and BL agency in his later years and also found time to create a veteran and vintage motorcycle collection. He passed away in January 1981, leaving his business to his staff, some of whom had spent their entire working lives with Munks.

Freddie Frith

Born in Grimsby in 1910; Lincolnshire stonemason Freddie Frith's racing career followed a typical pattern for young men with racing aspirations; becoming involved in trials and club events during the late 1920s. He was usually Velocette-mounted and in 1930 he made his Isle of Man debut, which was a portent of a brilliant career when he rode a dealer-sponsored KTT into third place in the Junior Manx Grand Prix. In 1932 he switched to a Norton and gained fifth place in the Senior Manx; this was a commendable effort, for he was riding a 350cc machine in a 500 cc race. His perseverance in the Manx series culminated in 1935 with a win in the Junior event and second place in the Senior behind J.K. Swanston who was a consistent Manx competitor and also a medical practitioner.

Not surprisingly Frith was recruited into the 1936 Norton work's team; a situation he justified with a win in the Junior and third place in a hard-fought Senior behind Jimmie Guthrie and Stanley Woods (Velocette). Another highlight for Frith was a decisive Senior Ulster win and a record lap of 95 mph. The 1937 TT series provided its own drama following a Norton 1-2-3 in the Junior result for Guthrie, Frith and White. Friday's Senior saw Guthrie assuming a comfortable lead until lap five when he retired at the Cutting, which later became the site of the Guthrie Memorial. With Guthrie's retirement, Woods inherited the lead, and try as he might he was unable to hold off a last lap challenge from Frith, who posted a record lap of 90 mph on his way to victory.

Following the TT the Norton team contested the classic Grands Prix, the Swiss, Dutch and Belgian; it was at the German Grand Prix that Guthrie crashed fatally at the final corner when firmly in the lead. The tragedy was compounded by the realization that Guthrie intended to retire at the end of the season.

During 1938 and 1939 it was mainly the Norton team which upheld British prestige in the 500cc class. By then BMW had achieved the reliability to win Grand Prix events; with Georg Meier becoming European Champion for 1938. In 1939 he became the first foreign rider to win a Senior TT on a foreign machine, while in second place was an Englishman, the burly Jock West also on a BMW and in third place was Freddie Frith. The 1939 Ulster TT was a resounding success for Serafini on the supercharged Gilera, while his greatest challenge came from a gallant Freddie Frith who brought his Norton home in second place. The Ulster was the final road race in a fabulous decade and apart from an entry at a post-war Shelsley Walsh hill-climb it was Frith's last race appearance on a works Norton.

Following army service, in 1947 Frith made a return to the TT, with a Junior Velocette and a Senior Guzzi; however a practice crash sidelined him from the TT and other classics. He made a return to racing at the 1947 Ulster GP and in his efforts to hold off a strong Norton challenge his Velocette suffered a broken valve.

The following year, 1948, his TT entries were a Junior Velocette and a Grand Prix Triumph for the Senior. This resulted in a comprehensive Junior win and retirement in the Senior. In 1949 he gained another victory in the Junior TT riding the new twin camshaft Velocette, after withstanding a strong challenge from AJS stars, Les Graham and Bill Doran.

This was also the inaugural year of the World Championships, and with victories at the TT and in every classic 350cc race, Frith and Velocette were undisputed winners in that category. At the end of the season he announced his retirement and the following year he was awarded an OBE for services to motor racing. The modest Grimsby man opened a successful motorcycle business in that area. Freddie Frith died in May 1988, a respected member of those inaugural World Champions.

Murray McLeod

Harold Daniell

Londoner Harold Daniell's racing career was remarkable in that it began in the early 1930s and continued into the post war era.

His initial racing forays began at English circuits, such as Donington Park and Syston Park. Daniell was fortunate in having his Nortons prepared by his brother-in-law, Steve Lancefield who was also a capable rider, however his real talents lay in race tuning.

They made quite a formidable duo on the race circuits and Harold became a consistent winner at Crystal Palace and other venues. In 1932 Daniell was runner up in the Senior Manx Grand Prix and a win in the Manx invariably led to an invitation to join a works team.

Daniell's perseverance was rewarded with victory in the 1933 Senior, however the magical invitation from Joe Craig was not forthcoming. Instead Harold became an AJS team member from 1934 to 1936 which proved to be a rather bleak period for the bespectacled Londoner.

AJS were developing a supercharged 500cc V4 that was shaping up as a liability rather than a winner. Their 350 'R' series single was only slightly more reliable and gave Harold just one T.T. finish from his six AJS starts with an eighth place in the 1935

Junior.

His AJS tenure had been most unrewarding and in 1937 he was entered for the TT on Lancefield-prepared Nortons. This was a most gratifying exercise for them both with Harold finishing in fifth place in both the Junior and Senior events, the first private entrant behind the works teams.

Joe Craig could scarcely continue to ignore his abilities and later in the season he was recruited into the works team. Harold's first appearance was in the 500cc class of the Dutch TT, partnering Guthrie who retired while leading the race.

The finishing order was Gall (BMW) in first place followed by Daniell after a most consistent ride. Two weeks later in the 350 class of the German Grand Prix Harold scored his first works victory ahead of team mate John White. Any satisfaction was later soured by Guthrie's tragic death in the Senior event.

For the 1938 season the Norton team comprised Harold Daniell, Freddie Frith and John White. The work's machines had undergone major changes since 1937, the obvious external difference was telescopic forks to replace the traditional girders.

Extensive testing was carried out at the Donington

Park circuit and Harold's teammates were generally enthusiastic about the arrangement despite the lack of damping and limited movement.

However Harold held strong reservations about the changes and felt more at ease using a Lancefield-prepared practice hack at the TT.

He recorded some impressive times with it but during a practice session he crashed in spectacular fashion. The bike was destroyed and Harold was more knocked about than he dared to admit.

The 1938 Junior TT gave Woods his ninth TT win, backed up by teammate Ted Mellors. Meanwhile Friday's Senior race was shaping up to be one of the most exciting in years. Norton's most serious challenge was expected to come from Georg Meier on a work's BMW and Velocette-mounted Stanley Woods.

Meier was in the process of changing a spark plug on the BMW at the warm-up period when he stripped the thread of the cylinder head. Retirement was the only option which saw Meier become a spectator from the grandstand.

BMW's 1938 foray had proved to be disastrous when during practice Meier's teammate Karl Gall crashed heavily and fractured his skull.

He returned to the Island for the 1939 TT series, only to crash again in practice, this time fatally.

Previous year's winner Frith set a cracking pace from the outset and until lap five he held a narrow lead over Woods on the Velocette. On lap six a relentless Woods assumed first place and seemed poised for a Velocette victory.

It was not to be. Daniell had not featured strongly in the opening stages and on the seventh circuit he came through with a record lap of 91 mph to beat the Irishman by sixty seconds. This was a remarkable win for Harold when one considers his practice crash and lack of time to familiarize himself with his actual race bike.

In the Junior TT of the following year the situations were reversed. Despite Daniell recording the fastest lap at 85 mph, it was Woods who came through to score his tenth TT victory. The winning margin was a mere 28 seconds after three hours and ten minutes of inspired riding.

This was Stanley Woods' final year of road racing, while for the remarkable Harold Daniell there were still triumphant years as a Norton teamster ahead of him.

The outbreak of war in September 1939 put an end

to any racing activities, much to the disappointment of many aspiring riders.

Harold was keen to enlist in the armed forces, and then to his dismay he was rejected on the grounds of defective eyesight, which seems rather ironic that the current holder of the lap record on the Isle of Man was deemed unfit for military service.

Eight long years were to elapse before Harold resumed an interrupted career where once again he was in the top echelon of road racing.

Murray McLeod

John White

By the late 1980s there was just one remaining member of the elite 1930s Norton works team. He was John White the Cambridge graduate who rode Nortons from 1935 to 1939. Born in Radlett Hertfordshire John White became involved with motorcycling from an early age.

His inspiration to ride in the Isle of Man came from fellow student Malcolm Muir. Both were members of the Cambridge University Auto Club and following Muir's win in the 1931 Senior Manx Grand Prix White made the decision to ride in the 1932 event.

Somehow he scraped together the forty-five pounds required to purchase a second hand KTT Velocette, which was a sizeable sum in those days; although it was not an auspicious debut for the newcomer. In the Junior race he came off on two occasions and eventually retired.

He returned the following year with a much-improved KTT and on it he led the Junior Manx, lapping at a record 75mph. Once again he was forced to retire, following a crash on the Mountain climb at the Gooseneck. White rode the 350 Velo in the 500 event and distinguished himself by finishing fifth, even after two crashes during the race.

As a result of these off-road aberrations his university chums labeled him 'Crasher' White, which was a somewhat unfair appellation that continued throughout his career.

Nortons were sufficiently impressed with White's rides to provide machines for the 1934 Manx. At the time British factories all signed a bond that they would not support riders in the Manx, but as White commented .... *the ink was hardly dry before Nortons broke the agreement.*

White had his first Manx success on Nortons with a win in the Junior event, but things did not go smoothly in the Senior. White led the race until he was halted briefly to replace a spark plug lead that had come adrift. Determined to make up the lost time he came off in a big way at Union Mills and considering his speed was in the vicinity of 100 mph he was fortunate to walk away from it.

Nevertheless John White became a member of the 1935 works team. At the time he was a biology master at Lydney Grammar School and was fortunate in having an indulgent Headmaster who allowed him time off to compete at the TT and the principal continental events.

His first outing was the Leinster in Ireland which was treated by the factories as a warm up event before the TT. When his works bike did not arrive in time for practice he was obliged to use his own hack Norton. As a result he began the race on an unfamiliar factory machine and crashed out. The bike was damaged which infuriated Joe Craig who wanted to drop him from the team for the forthcoming TT.

Craig relented to the extent of providing a bike for the Junior, but pointedly not the Senior. White finished third in the Junior, behind team mates Guthrie and Rusk; and despite his Junior placing he was not included in the team for the German and Swiss Grands Prix. He did get a bike for the Belgian Junior Grand Prix which he won with a record lap at 84 mph.

For 1936 White was again a Norton team member and with no restrictions as to where he could ride. This was the year that Nortons appeared with rear springing on their works machines and riders were all agreed that it contributed significantly to comfort and handling. Freddie Frith scored a convincing win in the Junior TT on the new model and backing him up in second place was John White.

At the Dutch TT White reversed the situation, finishing first ahead of Frith. At the Ulster Grand Prix Frith scored an emphatic win in the 500 race;

while in the 350 Ulster which was run concurrently with the Senior White fought a tremendous battle with Ted Mellors on a works Velocette.

White crashed on the fourth lap and Mellors retired with chain trouble, leaving the way clear for eventual winner Ernie Thomas on a second works Velo.

White's 1937 TT resulted in third place in both the Junior and Senior; and following the TT, White repeated his Dutch TT win, setting up a lap record which stood for the ensuing twelve years.

The following year 1938, was memorable for Harold Daniell's record-breaking Senior, while the consistent White finished fourth in both the Junior and Senior events.

With Nortons gearing up for war production they pulled out of racing for 1939; however at the last minute they provided machines for Frith, Daniell and White. Earlier White had obtained a Junior entry with NSU, however the unwieldy supercharged twin never impressed during practice and expired early in its race. His Senior Norton nevertheless took him to a creditable fifth place.

White scored his last race win at the 1939 French Grand Prix, which was held at Rheims and was not a fully supported event. Shortly afterwards war was declared and despite being in a reserved occupation White joined the ranks of experienced motorcycle instructors; finishing the war as a captain in the engineers. He never raced again. By that time he had married and did not consider racing to be a suitable occupation for a married man.

John White's TT record with Nortons was a model of reliability with eight finishes from eight starts, the majority of them on the leader board. His sole TT retirement was the 1939 Junior when his blown NSU expired early in the race.

He remembered his teammates with affection, particularly Guthrie and Frith but with reservations about Daniell. His only regret was that he would have preferred to ride for Velocette. In his opinion they would not have restricted his race appearances the way Norton did. They may have even paid him a salary which Norton never did.

Maurice Cann

Some riders forged successful careers on a variety of makes, often on their path to a place on a work's team. Others are remembered for their absolute loyalty to one make; Norton team rider Johnnie Lockett is a perfect example of this, during a career that was 100% Norton.

Leicester's Maurice Cann did have an early involvement with a variety of makes; however his notable successes were centred on 250cc Guzzis.

When one considers that he was a private entrant, Cann enjoyed remarkable success in post-war classic races, including a first place at the 1948 Lightweight TT, plus five wins at the Ulster Grand Prix. Four of these were in succession,1947-1950, and significantly the 1952 race, the last occasion when it was run on the old Clady circuit, before its move to Dundrod.

Born in Leicester in 1911, Maurice Cann developed an early interest in motorcycles, and while still at school he owned his fist bike, an extremely rare shaft-drive Belgian FN.

His competition career began at age 17, with an involvement in local trials and grass track events on a KNS Velocette. He became a consistent performer on the Velo at the abbreviated Syston Park circuit, until its closure around 1932.

Circuits such as these nurtured the careers of many riders, Maurice Cann included.

As a result of his efforts there and later at Donington Park, he won a free entry to the 1931 Manx Grand Prix

In company with brother Tom and their friend Austin Munks, another of Syston's top riders, the trio made their debut at the 1931 Manx. Austin Munks went on to success in future Manx series, and despite the loss of an eye in a shooting accident, he won the 1935 Junior and completed the double in 1936.

Maurice Cann's 1931 Manx debut resulted in a Junior retirement, while on the same 350 Velocette he finished 9th in the Senior. After a three year lapse he made a return to the Manx in 1935, this time Norton-mounted, which brought more positive results, with 7th in the Junior and 10th in the Senior.

The following year was unproductive, with retirements in both races; however in 1937 Cann's efforts were rewarded with a pleasing Manx double, with rising star Ken Bills second to Cann in both races. His love affair with Guzzis began in 1937, with the acquisition of the 250 that Paddy Johnston finished 8th in the 1931 Lightweight TT.

In spite of its rather ancient format; the veteran Guzzi caused much consternation among the established stars at Donington Park and other venues in the years leading up to the war.

Cann's war years were involved in armaments production for the Royal Navy, and during that period, in anticipation of racing being resumed, he designed and built in his home workshop, a twin-cam conversion for his own Norton. With the return of the TT series in 1947, the Cann Norton made a promising debut at the Junior TT.

Until lap three it held second place behind eventual winner Bob Foster, who led throughout on his Velocette. Cann's home-brewed Norton proved faster than the work's models, until his unfortunate retirement on lap three.

His prospects for Wednesday's Lightweight TT were far more promising, with his main opposition expected to come from Irish rider Manliff Barrington, whose entrant was his countryman, the legendary Stanley Woods.

From the outset, the Cann/Barrington pair became involved in a race-long duel, with Cann leading until lap six, when he stopped to change a hairpin valve spring, a common problem on Guzzis at the time.

Barrington gained a two second lead until lap seven, when by virtue of his early start number (No.3) Cann crossed the finish line, followed later by Barrington.

Amateur time-keepers were all agreed that Cann's lap seven effort placed him ahead of Barrington, however the official time-keepers decreed otherwise and declared Barrington the winner. Protests flowed thick and fast, but the ACU never admitted that their time-keepers had blundered.

The following year Cann was vindicated to some extent at the Lightweight TT, which on this occasion was a massed start. The early laps saw a spirited Cann/Barrrington duel, until the Irishman's race ended in retirement.

Cann then cruised to an emphatic win, finishing ten minutes ahead of second-placed Roland Pike on an elderly Rudge. Cann's Junior TT also proved rewarding with his 5th place on one of the newly-introduced AJS 7Rs in their TT debut.

A massed-start was again used in 1950, and from the outset, Cann was involved in a race-long duel with Italian champion Dario Ambrosini on the Benelli.

The result remained in doubt until the final

seconds when Ambrosini out-sprinted Cann to the chequered flag to win by the barest of margins. Later that year, the battling duo contested the 250 Ulster Grand Prix, where Cann managed to reverse the TT result, to score his fourth consecutive win there. Maurice retained in interest in historic racing and made parade appearances up to the time of his death in February 1989.

Murray McLeod

Dennis Parkinson

Reviewing the careers of those riders who remained loyal to the Manx Grand Prix; few if any can match that of Dennis Parkinson.

Beginning in 1932 his Manx appearances extended to 1953, the year of his retirement, a period when he recorded five wins, and in all categories.

From Wakefield, Yorkshire, Parkinson made his Manx debut in 1932; his Norton finishing 29th in the Junior.

The following year, 1933, his Junior OK Supreme took him to 23rd and the Senior Norton to 22nd. From 1934 to 1935 he persevered in all three classes, with three finishes and three retirements.

In 1936 Parkinson recorded the first of three consecutive Lightweight victories, riding an Excelsior Manxman. The Manxman was marketed in three capacities; 250, 350 and 500cc, with the 250 by far the most competitive.

In 1937 he scored another Lightweight win, and in the process became the first rider to gain a Junior replica on a Lightweight machine.

The 1938 series saw a Junior/Senior double for Ken Bills, on Nortons prepared by Steve Lancefield, and a third Lightweight win for Parkinson.

With the return of the series in 1946, many of the pre-war riders resumed their interrupted careers, including Dennis Parkinson, who performed steadily to claim third in the Junior and fourth in the Senior.

For the 1947 season Parkinson approached famed technician Francis Beart with a proposal that Beart prepare his machines for the forthcoming events.

First on the calendar were a series of airfield meetings, plus short circuit venues like Brough and Scarborough.

Their first Isle of Man appointment was the newly-instituted Clubman's TT, in which Parkinson was entered in the Junior on an International Norton. Dennis scored a convincing win, at a race average of 70.74mph.

Their next major venture was the September Manx series, where Dennis would ride his own 500 Norton in the Senior and Beart's 350 Norton in the Junior.

Of the race itself, Eric Briggs went on to dominate both events, where in the Junior; Dennis was holding second place until the final lap when he wetted a spark plug at Governors Bridge and had to push his machine home to finish fourth.

His Senior race had a more positive outcome, with a handy second place behind Briggs and ahead of veteran rider Albert Moule.

The following year, 1948, Parkinson had the satisfaction of a win in the Junior Manx, again on a Beart-prepared Norton.

The race itself was laced with excitement from start to finish, initially with Parkinson holding an early lead until lap two, when he was overtaken by Geoff Duke, riding in his very first road race.

Duke had the misfortune to retire on lap four with a split oil tank, an old Norton failing.

Parkinson now had to contend with challenges from Reg Armstrong, Phil Heath and Don Crossley. After putting up the fastest lap at 79.54, Armstrong also retired, leaving the way clear for Parkinson to score a pleasing win ahead of Phil Heath (AJS) and Don Crossley (Velocette).

This was a good result for the Beart/Parkinson duo, which represented the first of many Manx successes for Francis Beart.

From the mid-1930's to the mid-1970's he gained a noteworthy reputation in his preparation of race machinery; a period when Beart-prepared bikes recorded impressive Manx results of eleven 1st places, ten 2nd, five 3rd and four 4th. Immaculately presented in that distinctive apple green finish, they could be regarded as racers *par excellence*, and in concourse condition.

Thus far Parkinson had recorded three Lightweight and one Junior Manx win, and from 1949 to 1953, the eventual year of his retirement he was focused on that elusive Senior Trophy.

Following a third place in the 1951 Senior Manx, in 1953 the dream became a reality, with a close-fought Senior win against two aspiring riders, Bob Keeler (Norton) and Derek Ennett (Matchless G45).

Although retired from racing, Dennis acted for a time as travelling marshal, utilizing his encyclopedic knowledge of a course he so often contested.

To the dismay of a host of friends and enthusiasts, Dennis passed away March 2004.

The MANX Grand Prix

Kenneth Bills

World War 2 had the effect of curtailing the careers of so many riders. At the cessation of hostilities those riders able to, went on to resume their interrupted vocation. Freddie Frith and Harold Daniell were two stars who went on to major achievements in the immediate post-war years.

One rider who was denied a more rewarding career was Kenneth Bills. An optician by profession, Ken Bills' first Island venture was the 1934 Manx Grand Prix. On a 250 Rudge he finished in fifth place in the Lightweight with a seventh berth in the Senior on a Vincent HRD. Bills persevered each year at the Manx and in 1938 he was rewarded with a Junior/Senior double, riding machines prepared by Norton specialist, Steve Lancefield. In more peaceful times a win in the Manx invariably led to a place in the Norton works team.

Unfortunately for Bills, Europe was building up to a world war and besides, Nortons were heavily involved in war production and not officially supporting racing in 1939. Tensions in Europe were inexorably building up to crisis point and somewhat optimistically the Manx Motorcycle Club pressed on with plans to run their Grand Prix in September.

On 1 September Germany invaded Poland; Britain's ultimatum to Germany expired on 3 September and as a result Britain declared war on Germany. Like many of his contemporaries, Ken Bills joined the RAF and qualified as a pilot.

After a lapse of 7 years and a concerted effort by the Manx Motorcycle Club racing was resumed in 1946. Some entrants were able to purchase what were virtually brand new Manx Nortons. In effect they were part of a batch of 1939 International Grand Prix models that were shipped as spares to the Isle of Man for the 1939 Manx Grand Prix. With the races cancelled the bikes were never used and were providentially stored out of harm's way in the Island.

Practice sessions for the 1946 Manx were generally restrained affairs; and. the weather was also un-co-operative, with rain and mist experienced for much of that pre-race period.

Ken Bills showed that he had lost none of his pre-war brilliance with a popular win in the Junior, and if the weather was inclement for the 350 race then the Senior was run in diabolical conditions. Dark horse for the race was Irishman Ernie Lyons, entered on a prototype Triumph twin. Mindful of the treacherous conditions and blissfully unaware of a broken frame he rode a masterly race to finish in first place ahead of the Nortons of Bills and Manx stalwart Harold Rowell.

Bills' impressive Manx record (3 wins, 3 seconds and a third spot) all on Nortons, secured him a place in the 1947 works team. The bikes were virtually the same as those campaigned by the 1938 team and required modifying to cope with the dreaded 'Pool' petrol. Craig's priority was to concentrate on the more prestigious Senior category.

This was borne out at the 1947 Junior where Velocette scored an emphatic 1-2-3-4, headed by veteran Bob Foster. Bills' was Norton's lone work's finisher in a lowly 21st position. His Senior mount expired on the last lap at Union Mills, his engine suffering from the effects of Pool; making it an inauspicious start to a season on works machinery, however his fortunes were about to improve markedly.

Spa Francorchamps was the venue for the 1947 Belgian Grand Prix and it was a foregone conclusion that Britain would dominate the Junior/Senior categories. It was in the 350 race that Norton sprang a surprise. After Norton's poor showing at the Junior TT it was expected that Velocette would continue their dominance at Spa; instead it proved to be Ken Bills' moment of triumph, leading the race from start to finish.

That particular 350 proved to be an absolute flier

and Norton teamster Ernie Lyons rode it in the 500 race and finished 8th, making him the first 350 rider home. The 350 Belgian was Bills' sole classic victory on a works Norton and until his retirement in 1950 he switched his allegiance to Velocettes in the 350 class and occasional outings on Triumphs in the 500 category. That was his format for the 1948 TT; a Velo for the Junior and a Grand Prix Triumph for the Senior, disappointingly neither went the distance. The Senior was remembered for its high attrition rate with just 23 finishers from 55 starters and of the six Triumphs contesting the Senior, none reached the finish line.

There were improved performances on the continent, particularly at the Belgian Grand Prix. Foster headed a Velocette 1-2-3 in the 350 race with Bills in fifth position behind Lockett's Norton. Five GP Triumphs started in the 500 event, won in stylish manner by Norton teamster, Lockett. Unlike the TT, every Triumph finished the race with Foster, Whitworth and Bills in 4th, 5th and 6th places. There was a better result for Bills at the Dutch TT where he scored a fine win for Velocette in the 350 event, after a race-long duel with Freddie Frith.

Bills' 1949 season began at the North West 200 in Northern Ireland, and also ended there following a crash in the latter stages. His swan song was the

1950 season which coincided with Norton's dominance of the Junior and Senior TT. Following Bob Foster's early retirement in the Junior TT, Velocette were never in the picture. Ken Bills' was the first Velo to finish; albeit in 9th place ahead of Norton stalwart Harry Hinton and Dave Whitworth in 11th on another Velocette.

There was a change of circumstances with Ken Bills' original Triumph entry in the Senior. In a bold move the Vincent factory entered their chief tester George Brown on a 500 Grey Flash, a race version of the Comet roadster. Brown had not fully recovered from the effects of an earlier crash at Eppynt in Wales and felt unfit to practice.

Bills took over Brown's entry and finished in 12th place, just missing out on a First Class replica. This was still a creditable performance on a machine that was more suited to short circuit racing, rather than an endurance event like the Isle of Man. Perhaps it was fitting that his career should finish on the same make on which he started back in 1934.

Murray McLeod

Ernie Lyons

Ever-smiling Ernie Lyons was generally associated with the Triumph marque. Riding the Coventry twins he scored some notable wins in his native Ireland and in the Isle of Man. Velocettes also featured in his road racing career, particularly during the 1949 season when he partnered Freddie Frith on Velos sponsored by Nigel Spring. During the 1948 season he made appearances on Moto Guzzis and AJS 7Rs.

His least successful season would have to be 1947, the year that he rode official Norton race ware. By all accounts it was a generally miserable period in the all-rounder's career.

Ernie's racing career began in 1932 while he was still at school. His first bike was a belt-drive 1912 Triumph which he campaigned despite its primitive design.

He later changed to a 1927 AJS and began to make his mark in local races. Apart from road racing he was also a successful trials and scrambles rider.

Anxious to graduate to a more sophisticated machine for the 1938 season, Ernie's had a preference for a new 'cammy' AJS; however with a price tag of £105, it was far beyond his resources. A better option was a new Triumph 'Speed Twin' that offered a similar performance and cost £75.

Ernie was able to purchase one for £64; the package coming as a collection of parts, minus electrics and mufflers. It turned out to be quite a successful race bike and one notable result was 2nd place at the 1938 N/W 200.

The highlight of Ernie's season was the 1938 Senior Manx Grand Prix and his first essay at that challenging circuit. His Triumph performed well during practice and on race day he was hoping for at least a favourable finish.

By all accounts it was a hectic race for Ernie Lyons. On several occasions he had minor skirmishes with corners and grass banks until he finally overdid things at the Gooseneck on his third lap and crashed out. Ernie was looking forward to a better showing at the 1939 Manx.

Unfortunately it was cancelled due to World War 2. It was a remarkable achievement for the Manx MCC to stage the 1946 series, following the conflict. Many of the pre-war riders were present, including the persistent Ernie Lyons.

Again he was entered on a Triumph twin and on this occasion he did enjoy factory support, albeit in a clandestine manner. Its engine was unique in that it was an all-alloy unit, similar in design to those fitted as generators to RAF wartime bombers.

Another feature was Triumph's patented sprung hub that served as an alternative form of rear suspension and a rather primitive one at that.

Ken Bills demonstrated that he had lost none of his pre-war brilliance with a win in the Junior Grand Prix. He was also a strong favourite for the Senior Grand Prix, a race that was made up almost entirely of Nortons.

The weather forecast was for wet conditions, prompting Lyons to fit a touring style front mudguard in place of the abbreviated racing pattern. This was clever foresight and was a contributing factor in his first place in the diabolical conditions that prevailed.

His win had the effect of forcing Triumph to somewhat reluctantly market a replica of Lyon's machine, which eventually emerged in 1948 as the Grand Prix; a fully-fledged racer that was available for the private entrant.

Manx baker Don Crossley won the 1948 Senior Manx on one and Kiwi Syd Jensen gained a creditable 5th place in the 1949 Senior TT. They proved to be generally unreliable in long-distance events and production was discreetly terminated in 1950.

Following the Manx Grand Prix, Ernie had further success at the prestigious Shelsley Walsh hill climb. He overcame a lack of practice to make FTD at a combined car and motorcycle meeting and in so doing he upset the car brigade considerably.

Yet despite Lyons' successes during 1946, Triumph management was implacably opposed to supporting an official works team.

Triumph's negative attitude prompted him to accept an offer to join Nortons for the forthcoming 1947 season, alongside veteran Harold Daniell and new star Artie Bell.

Ken Bills was also included in the team, with the understanding that he and Lyons were the junior members. Ernie featured on the leader board during practice for the TT, but race days proved disappointing.

He crashed out at the Gooseneck on the opening lap of the Junior and was pronounced unfit to start in the Senior at the Belgian Grand Prix on the following weekend he was confident of winning the 350 event and after only one lap his bike blew up.

He rode Ken Bills' 350 winner in the 500 race and came in 8th; the first 350 to finish.

Apart from a second place in the Senior Ulster

Grand Prix behind Artie Bell, it was a generally unproductive year for him on works Nortons.

For the 1948 TT he was entered for the Senior on a Moto Guzzi, sponsored by fellow Irishman Stanley Woods; plus a dealer-entered 7R AJS for the Junior. Lyons' teammate for the Senior was the Italian ace, Omobono Tenni and with the superior speed of the Guzzi both riders were potential winners.

Lyons made a meteoric start, only to run out of brakes and crash heavily at the Bungalow on his opening lap. Earlier in the week his AJS fractured a fuel line, which ended his Junior race at the Gooseneck.

It had been another disastrous TT week for Ernie Lyons but in the following year he had a remarkable change of fortune.

During the 1948-49 off-season, Velocette were burning the midnight oil, designing a new twin-camshaft version of the evergreen KTT. Eight 350s and two 500s were built and these were made available to selected riders.

Nigel Spring acquired a pair of 350s, plus the two 500s, to be ridden by Freddie Frith and Ernie Lyons. Frith took the new model to a win in the Junior TT, after an earlier challenge from AJS stars, Les

Graham and Bill Doran.

Lyons scored his highest-ever TT finish with a steady second place behind Frith. The 500s were not fancied as potential Senior winners yet once again Ernie Lyons made a leader-board finish with third place behind the Nortons of Harold Daniell and Johnnie Lockett.

A major disappointment to Velocette fans was Frith's third lap retirement in what proved to be his final Isle of Man appearance.

Ernie's final road race appearance was the 1950 Junior Ulster, riding a Velo from the Nigel Spring stable.

He was well placed in the early stages, battling for the lead with team mate Reg Armstrong and fellow Irishman Louis Carr on a works Norton. The situation was unfolding as a great day for the Irish but Ernie's race ended at Tully Corner, following a tangle with Bill Lomas on another Velocette.

Lomas was obviously not impressed with Ernie's actions and relayed his displeasure in no uncertain manner and on that note Ernie retired from the road racing scene. He continued to ride in trials and scrambles until 1963, the year he finally terminated a colourful racing career.

Ernie retired to a farm in County Kildare and by happy coincidence his property was sited next door to the farm on which he was born.

Eric Briggs

The careers of quite a few riders spanned the pre-war and post-war periods. Some continued their winning ways, typified by Ken Bills, Dennis Parkinson and Austin Munks, while other riders gained that elusive victory in the early post-war era. A classic example was Eric Briggs from Bradford, whose Manx forays began in 1938, where the series was dominated by Ken Bills. Eric Briggs' Junior race gained him a worthy 5th place, while in the Senior he suffered a retirement.

The following year, 1939 was an uneasy period internationally, with rumours and threats of war; nevertheless the Manx MCC proceeded with plans to hold the Manx GP in that September. Following Britain's declaration of war on 3 September it proved to be the event that never was. Six long years of brutal conflict changed the face of Europe and the world, and in an era of extreme austerity it was something of a minor miracle for the Manx MCC to hold the 1946 Manx GP. Regrettably many of the old faces were missing; however some of the stalwarts had returned and Eric Briggs was one of that number.

Practice periods were generally restrained affairs; with vital components like spark plugs and tyres in short supply this was not the time to be chasing records. The weather too was unco-operative, with rain and mist for most of the practice sessions, and if the weather was inclement for the Junior race, then the Senior was run in diabolic conditions. Eric Briggs started in both races and unfortunately both ended in retirements.

Looking forward to better results in 1947, Eric was an entrant in the inaugural Clubmen's TT series, run as part of the 1947 TT event. Here was a chance for clubmen to face the challenge of the TT course, riding standard machines rather then pukka road racers. The opportunity for clubmen to compete on road bikes had its genesis at the 1938 Donington Day, a pre-war event staged by Motorcycling's editor Graham Walker, so the 1947 Clubmen's series could be regarded as an extension of that Donington event.

With post-war motorcycle production unable to match demand, many clubmen were obliged to revert to pre-war machinery, which was no handicap to Eric Briggs with his borrowed 1939 International Norton. He led throughout, with Yorkshire all-rounder Allan Jefferies on a Triumph Tiger 100 finishing second. Equipped with a brace of new Manx Nortons, prepared by Steve Lancefield, Briggs no doubt faced the 1947 Manx GP with confidence. This was forcibly demonstrated in the Junior GP, where Briggs led from start to finish; however the Senior was a close-run affair with Dennis Parkinson maintaining the lead until lap three when Briggs made his challenge, taking the lead, which he held to the finish. Just 50 seconds separated winner Briggs from Parkinson, with another Manx veteran Albert Moule in third place.

A win in the Manx generally led to a place in the Norton team, and in Briggs' situation he was on works machinery for the 1948 TT series. Monday's Junior TT was dominated by the rapid Velocettes of Frith and Foster, with Artie Bell's Norton in third place; while Briggs finished sixth among the AJS and Norton works riders. Friday's Senior was remembered for its high attrition rate; with Artie Bell the lone finisher of the Norton works riders, albeit in first place.

Briggs' future TT outings were private entries, and in 1949 he secured 9th place on a Velocette in the Junior TT. In 1950 he recorded his last TT finish and for the remainder of his career (1949-50) he participated in the Continental Circus, a Gypsy existence for those hardy riders, racing on weekends from one venue to another, relying on start money plus the odd bonuses from the oil and accessory barons to scrape out a somewhat precarious career.

Murray McLeod

Cromie McCandless

Born January 1921 Cromie McCandless was the younger brother of the innovative engineer Rex McCandless; Cromie as the name implies hailed from Ireland; Belfast to be precise.

In partnership with Norton team member and dual TT winner Artie Bell, Rex created an engineering enterprise in Belfast that was host to a range of forward-thinking projects.

One that merits inclusion was the so-called 'Featherbed' frame which extended the competitiveness of the racing Norton into the late 1950's, until it was overwhelmed by the latest Italian designs which were to dominate the racing scene into the 1960's.

Rex McCandless was also a competent rider, an all-rounder in the early post-war years; however it was Cromie who left a greater imprint on the road racing scene, in a career extending from 1947 to his retirement in 1952.

Cromie's Manx GP tenure ran from 1947 to 1949, always on Junior and Senior Nortons, but sadly his 1947 and 1948 series were littered with retirements.

However in 1949 his Manx prospects improved markedly, with legendary race technician Francis

Beart acting as Cromie's entrant.

The taciturn, unflappable Beart had forged a worthy reputation in pre-war days, notably at Brooklands and other speed venues.

His first Manx venture was the 1938 series where he prepared the Nortons for rising star Johnny Lockett, who led the Senior race in its early stages, before sundry problems reduced him to second at the finish, behind Manx veteran Ken Bills.

Post-war, Beart resumed an interrupted career which brought him in contact with many aspiring riders.

The Beart/McCandless duo had its beginnings in 1948, with Francis preparing machines for local Irish and UK mainland events to extend Cromie's burgeoning career.

In 1948 Francis had the satisfaction of a Junior Manx GP win, with Dennis Parkinson the rider; and with the approach of the 1949 series his focus was on a Senior win or possibly a Junior/Senior double, this time with Cromie as his favoured rider.

Consensus of opinion was that Cromie's greatest challenge would come from Geoff Duke, who was enjoying a successful season in local events, plus a Senior Clubman's TT win at the Isle of Man in June.

The Junior Manx developed into a see-sawing contest, with first Duke assuming the lead only to have to yield to McCandless in the latter stages. Duke had the misfortune to be baulked by a slower rider at Ramsey Hairpin and was brought down.

He did restart and pressed on to the finish to come second to McCandless who rode a fine race, during which he raised the lap record to 83.48 mph.

Conditions for the Senior race were nigh on perfect and once again it was a torrid Duke/McCandless battle, with both riders breaking the lap record as the race progressed.

McCandless had gained the lead on the final lap, only to run out of fuel at Cronk-ny-Mona, but by pushing the Norton up a bank he managed to coax enough fuel to the back of the tank to continue.

This unscheduled stop cost him thirty seconds, but at least he made it the finish, albeit in second place to Duke.

The 1949 Manx was a mix of triumph and disappointment for the Beart/McCandless duo; however Francis was keen to have Cromie as his rider for the 1950 season, in particular for the local Irish races.

For 1951 their focus was on the TT, where Francis

was preparing machines for Cromie and veteran rider Tommy McEwan.

The Junior TT was a predictable Duke win at record speed, while Cromie finished in 7th place, the first private runner behind the official Norton and AJS teams and Bob Foster's Velocette.

Cromie was paid a rare compliment with the offer of a place in the Norton team for Friday's Senior TT, which he repaid with a fine third place behind Geoff Duke and AJS star Bill Doran.

Aside from his Norton entries, Cromie was also a member of the Italian Mondial team, making an appearance at the inaugural 125cc TT; with Cromie winning comprehensively in a 1-2-3 Mondial finish; while at the Ulster Grand Prix he scored another win for Mondial, who went on to claim the manufacturer's championship, with Carlo Ubbiali crowned World Champion.

His last race win was at the 1952 Senior Ulster, this time aboard a works Gilera. Initially he was offered a works ride from Norton, but to their disappointment he accepted the Gilera offer.

This was also the final year the event was held on the original Clady circuit, before the move to Dundrod. Cromie rode a heroic race, matching the challenges from Les Graham, Ken Kavanagh and other stars to emerge as a worthy winner, and on that note Cromie McCandless retired from the racing scene.

He passed away in January 1992, aged 71.

Murray McLeod

Geoff Duke

Born at St. Helens, Lancashire in 1923, Geoffrey Duke was a comparatively late starter in motorcycle competition. During his military tenure with the Royal Corps of Signals he was an enthusiastic member of their motorcycle display team. Following his demob in 1947 he purchased a 350 competition BSA, and on the 'Beeza' he began his career as a trials rider.

Duke's exploits attracted the attention of Artie Bell who was instrumental in obtaining a position for him at Norton, At first he had scant success with the 500T, which was quite a deal heavier than the BSA, however the prospect of becoming involved in road racing seemed more appealing. Norton supported him fully, to the extent of loaning a 350 Manx racer for the forthcoming 1948 Manx Grand Prix.

He had applied earlier for an entry for the 1948 Clubman's TT, but with the event oversubscribed his entry was rejected. His next option was the September Manx series, which would be his first ever road race. Duke arrived in the Island a week before official practice began, and using his trials bike fitted with road tyres he set about learning that most challenging circuit.

Duke's practice plan was to conserve his machine on the straights and concentrate on the quickest possible way through the corners; as a result he did not feature on the practice leader board; however on race day he faced the starter, confident of at least a good showing.

Race favourite was Dennis Parkinson, riding a Beart-prepared Norton. Parkinson was already a triple winner at pre-war Manx events; meantime Duke ignored such reputations and rode to a pre-determined plan, which saw him assume the lead on lap three. Into his fourth lap Duke had the misfortune to experience the old Norton bogey of a split oil tank. Retirement was the only option, which was a great disappointment, as he may well have won a Manx Grand Prix at his first attempt.

Duke's first Isle of Man success was the 1949 Senior Clubman's TT, where he was entered on a Norton International. He dominated the race from start to finish and in the process created a lap record which stood until 1953.

Throughout 1949 Duke took part in mainland and Irish events; one of these was the 350 class of the North West 200, where he finished a handy third behind TT legends, Harold Daniell and Freddie Frith. However at the Skerries 100 in July he crashed out, sustaining a broken leg and painful lacerations when he was thrown through a thicket hedge.

Duke had barely recovered from his injuries when practice began for the 1949 Manx Grand Prix. Consensus of opinion was that Duke's main opposition would be from Cromie McCandless on Beart-prepared Nortons, which was how it eventuated.

The Junior race was a close-fought affair, with Duke holding a slender lead over McCandless until lap four, when Duke was forced to lay his Norton down at Ramsey Hairpin to avoid a bunch of slower riders. Despite some damage he managed to restart and finish the race second to McCandless.

The situation was reversed in the Senior race, with McCandless suffering fuel shortage while leading on his final lap. He was able to re-start, however the thirty second hold-up reduced him to second place behind Duke.

Following his Manx success Duke was an obvious selection for the 1950 works team. His initial outing was in late 1949 at the Montlhery speed bowl near Paris for the purpose of attacking some current world records. Artie Bell was Duke's partner in the attempts which resulted in a bag of 21 records.

To be included in the Norton team on equal terms with Bell, Daniell and Lockett was really special and to start the 1950 season on the new-look

'Featherbed' was an opportunity beyond compare. Duke scored emphatic wins in the 500 class of the Senior TT, the Ulster Grand Prix and the final Grand Prix of the season, the Italian.

Only for tyre failure in Belgium and Holland he would have become 500cc World Champion at his first attempt. The following season he was doubly vindicated, becoming World Champion in both 350 and 500cc categories.

This was a remarkable achievement; in particular to claim the 500 crown; riding a machine that was clearly slower than the Italian multis which were his main opposition. Duke remained loyal to Norton for the 1952 season and in spite of his undoubted ability it was obvious he was fighting a losing battle. He did gain the 350 World Title but by that stage the 500 Norton was quite outclassed.

Apart from that disappointing outcome, Duke was bewildered by Norton's attitude regarding his future prospects with them. In his three seasons with Norton he had ridden brilliantly to gain 3 World Championships for the firm.

Then at the start of the 1953 season Nortons announced to the Press; "There is no place for Duke in the Norton team." Later, Duke discovered that the objection to his re-joining the team came from his old teammate Ken Kavanagh.

If Norton did not want Duke's services, then Gilera were more than anxious to sign him and with a retainer and benefits that made Norton's salary look decidedly paltry. It was the commencement of a 5-year tenure with the Italian firm, which gained the St. Helens star a further 3 World Championships, (1953-54-55) including the 1955 Senior TT at record speed.

Duke's final season was in 1959 riding Manx Nortons. This was also his Isle of Man swansong where he gained a doughty 4th place in that year's Junior II. His last race wins were in September at the non-championship Swiss Grand Prix at Locarno where he scored a Junior/Senior double, plus a Lightweight win on a 250 works Benelli; following which he announced his retirement from motorcycle racing.

The 'Duke' still made parade appearances, where a younger generation had the opportunity to witness one of the truly greats in action.

David Bennett

Dave Bennett's tenure as a Norton team member was tragically brief, nevertheless he merits an inclusion in this volume. He was born in Birmingham in 1928, the youngest of three brothers. With Stan and Clive employed at Ariel Motorcycles it was inevitable that Dave would pursue a similar career.

His duties at Ariel were mundane to start with and later he became involved in road testing, which proved to be a much more enjoyable experience for the enthusiastic teenager.

On his 18th birthday Dave began his stint of compulsory National Service, and after basic training he was posted to Tel el Kebir in Egypt. Off duty periods were occupied with speedway racing on heavily modified army bikes.

With his National Service completed Dave returned to his old employer Ariel who supported him in national trials and scrambles. One highlight was the 1949 International Six Day's Trial, held that year in Wales. He was poised to win a Gold Medal but was forced to retire on the fifth day.

Despite his trials success, Bennett was determined to move on to road racing. In late 1949 he secured a position at Norton where his growing reputation earned him a place in the race shop. This was satisfying work but the low wages ruled out any hope of purchasing competitive race machines. It was the intervention of family friend Ernie Earles that hoisted Dave on the first rung of the racing ladder; with Earles providing a 350 and 500 Manx Norton for Dave to ride in the 1950 season.

The new 'Featherbed' model did not become available to private owners until 1951, so for the 1950 season it would have to be the outmoded 'Garden Gate' version for Bennett and other aspiring riders.

He campaigned the Nortons at a variety of circuits during the year; the high-light of which was the 1950 Manx Grand Prix. The newcomer featured regularly on the practice leader board and on race days he was a model of consistency.

Veteran Don Crossley on a 7R AJS won the Junior after a spirited tussle with Peter Romaine and Robin Sherry and almost unnoticed after a steady ride was Dave Bennett in 8th place. Favourite for the Senior was Peter Romaine on the Beart-prepared Norton, who held off various challenges to lead throughout. In second place was Mick Featherstone with Harold Clark third and after another steady ride was Dave Bennett. Norton machines occupied the first fifteen places.

Following his encouraging Manx performances, Bennett's main focus for 1951 was the Manx Grand Prix. Once again Ernie Earles provided new bikes, in this instance a brace of 'Featherbed' Nortons. Despite Bennett's connection with Norton's race shop, both were completely standard and not thinly disguised specials.

During practice for the Manx, Bennett featured strongly in both 350 and 500 sessions. Favourite for the Junior event was Robin Sherry on a rapid 7R AJS which in all probability was a works special.

Bennett made a strong challenge to Sherry throughout the race, holding second place until the fourth lap when he retired with a broken primary chain.

Inclement weather forced an overnight postponement of the Senior, however race day was sunny but strong winds could prove bothersome at exposed parts of the circuit. From the start Bennett went into an early lead which he maintained throughout.

In second place was Don Crossley on a Beart-Norton and in third was Robin Sherry on a prototype Matchless G45 twin. Sherry was displaced at the finish by veteran Denis Parkinson on one of the swarms of Nortons that followed the

leader home

Following his record-breaking Manx win Dave Bennett had proved himself worthy of a place in the 1952 Norton works team. The newcomer would be partnering Geoff Duke and Reg Armstrong, although his first works outing was the 1951 autumn race meeting at the Thruxton circuit.

The 'Daily Express' Trophy final saw a titanic battle between Les Graham's MV and Dave Bennett's Norton, with the MV edging out Bennett's Norton and John Surtees' Vincent Grey Flash.

The opening Grand Prix of 1952 was the Swiss; with the Norton team on the line against a strong AJS works trio, plus the Gilera and MV entries. During practice it became apparent that the local fuel was not compatible with the works Nortons. Bennett's motor was affected more than his teammates' and required a complete re-build. This factor was to have disastrous consequences for Bennett.

The 500cc GP began at a furious rate and saw Duke holding first place ahead of Graham, Brett and Coleman with Bennett in mid-field. It soon developed into a race of attrition.

Duke's Norton, which was not the subject of a re-build as was Bennett's, succumbed to the damage caused by the faulty fuel. As the race progressed there were further retirements and on lap 22 of the 28-lap race the order was Doran, Bennett and Brett. His was the lone works Norton battling with the more experienced AJS duo of Doran and Brett.

This developed into a fierce battle for the lead which changed repeatedly and with no quarter given.

As Doran and Brett sped past the pits on lap 27 there was no sign of Bennett. It was at first presumed that he too had suffered engine trouble but in his efforts to stay with the AJS pair he had run out of road, hit a tree and was killed instantly. It was a tragic circumstance. Only for that engine re-build following practice Bennett's Norton may well have expired as did Geoff Duke's, thereby saving him from that fatal crash.

A saddened Brett and Doran crossed the line in that order. Thus ended the all-too-brief career of a rider whom Geoff Duke described as having 'exceptional talent'.

Bob McIntyre

Few riders have earned greater respect than Glaswegian, Bob McIntyre, from fans and fellow riders alike.

During a road racing career that began in 1952 and was tragically ended in 1962, Bob 'Mac' had risen to the apex of his career with an Isle of Man double at the 1957 Golden Jubilee TT, and only for unfortunate circumstances could well have been that year's 500cc World Champion.

Born 28 November 1928 at Scotstoun, Glasgow, Robert McGregor McIntyre's competition career began in local scrambles in 1948, using his 350 Ariel Red Hunter road bike. After a few seasons of off-road competition he fulfilled an earlier ambition to go road racing, and significantly at the Isle of Man, a venue that would feature strongly in his racing future.

His Island debut was the 1952 Junior Clubman's TT, riding a 350 Gold Star BSA, a model that would eventually dominate clubman racing. During the race, Bob's machine was afflicted with a partially blocked carburetor jet, which reduced him to second place at the finish behind Eric Houseley's BSA.

His disappointment was eased somewhat by a win at the Junior Manx Grand Prix, riding a 7R AJS.

Riding the same 350 he finished second in the Senior Manx, headed only by Derek Farrant on the prototype G45 Matchless.

After competing at English and Scottish short circuit venues in 1953, Bob made his international debut at the North West 200 in Northern Ireland, again on the 7R. This resulted in a satisfying Junior win, and despite a retirement at the Isle of Man, his second place at the Junior Ulster and other events attracted the attention of AJS management, resulting in a place in the AJS works team for 1954.

His Junior TT ended in retirement; however his team mates, Rod Coleman and Derek Farrant finished first and second to record a pleasing result for AJS; their first win since Jimmie Guthrie's 1930 Lightweight victory.

The Senior TT, where Bob finished 14th was remembered as one of the most controversial ever; with the race being stopped after four laps, due to the appalling weather conditions.

Bob's sole AJS win was at the non-championship race at Pau, with a third at the Junior Ulster, plus 6th at the Belgian and Swiss Grands Prix. A significant aspect for the 1954 team was the final appearance of the troublesome 'Porcupine' twin, which despite earlier promise was never seriously raced again.

Bob's AJS tenure had proved less than memorable, and for 1955 he began an enduring association with Scots sponsor Joe Potts. Aside from his fine human qualities, Bob was a natural development engineer, with an uncanny instinct for visualizing an idea in theory and applying it in practice. Allied to this he was a gifted rider, with a will to win that was second to none.

He had a reputation for driving machinery too hard, but his supporters were unanimous in that he never over-revved an engine. Most riders experience a degree of ill-fortune, while in Bob Mac's situation he seemed to have had more than his fair share .

For 1955 the Potts' Equipe's preparations were focused on the Junior TT, for which a new 350 Manx Norton was purchased, and fitted with a full dustbin fairing was capable of 125mph; very good for a privately-prepared entry.

At the Junior TT, Bob was in superb form, leading the race for four laps, until sadly the Norton's performance began to fade, allowing Bill Lomas on the Guzzi to come through for a well-judged win.

After the race, motorcycle racer/journalist Vic Willoughby road-tested the Guzzi and the Norton, and was astounded that anyone could ride the

Norton in the state it was in, let alone almost win on it.

If 1956 was not entirely fruitful, then 1957 proved to be the highlight of Bob Mac's career, which came about through the influence of Gilera champion Geoff Duke. His team mate Reg. Armstrong had retired from racing at the end of 1956, thus leaving a vacancy in the team. Duke lobbied strongly to have McIntyre in the 1937 squad, and in this he was successful.

In Duke's estimation there was only one candidate with such natural ability, experience, combined with the right touch of restraint. Bob had previously turned down an offer of a Gilera ride in the 1956 TT, preferring to remain loyal to the Potts' stable.

Bob's Gilera debut was at Imola, an important meeting in the racing calendar prior to the TT. In both 350 and 500 events he more than justified his place in the Gilera squad by taking a commanding lead in both races, only to be delayed by ignition problems.

His Isle of Man excursions emphasized the brilliance of Bob McIntyre in scoring his own TT double. Bob's Junior TT provided moments of anxiety, when his Gilera went onto three cylinders on his second lap, necessitating a pit stop to change the offending spark plug.

From then on he was never headed, going on to score a convincing win, ahead of Aussie KeIth Campbell on a Guzzi and another Aussie, Bob Brown, recently recruited to the Gilera team in third.

His main opposition in Friday's Senior; extended to eight laps to commemorate the TT's Golden Jubilee, was expected to come from John Surtees on the MV, the strong Guzzi team, with Walter Zeller's BMW also a consideration.

From the outset, Bob stamped his authority on the race, leading throughout, and in the process breaking the magic 'ton' barrier, to finish at an average speed of 98.99mph. In second place was John Surtees on the unfaired Mv, with the reliable Bob Brown third.

The Dutch TT followed the Isle of Man, and in the 350 race Bob's powerful Gilera was narrowly beaten by the more nimble Guzzi of Keith Campbell. Bob's Senior race had an unfortunate outcome; no doubt feeling drained after his epic 350 race, plus the intense heat of the day, he unexpectedly ran out of road.

This unfortunate incident certainly scuttled his chances of winning the World's Championship, as he was unfit to contest the 500 Belgian Grand Prix, which was won in controversial manner by team mate Libero Liberati.

Still far from recovered, Bob contested the Ulster GP, and again his 350 aspirations were thwarted by ignition failure. In the Senior race, won by Liberati, Bob finished second ahead of Geoff Duke on the third Gilera.

The team then journeyed to Monza, to contest the Italian GP, which would see a resolution as to the World Championship winners. Liberati was well placed in the 500 category, while McIntyre was also poised to make his claim.

He scored a convincing win in the 350 race, but at the finish he was obviously quite unwell. Subsequent X-rays revealed a broken vertebra, previously undiagnosed, which had healed prior to Monza, only to have come unstuck during the 350 race.

This setback put paid to further racing during what was left of the season. Liberati went on to win the 500 race and subsequently the championship, ahead of the Gileras of Duke and Milani.

In November 1957, with racing over, Gilera mounted an attempt on the one hour record at the Monza track. McIntyre's ride on the 350 Gilera was a heroic effort, considering the extremely bumpy surface, during which he averaged 141 mph.

His record stood until 1964, when Mike Hailwood on the 500 MV Agusta raised it to 144 mph on the Daytona speed bowl in Florida.

At season's end came the bombshell, that by mutual agreement all the Italian factories would no longer support racing, due to the prohibitive costs involved. This included Gilera, Moto Guzzi, MV Agusta, Mondial and others, while for current works riders, this decision virtually ended many careers.

Then rather brazenly, in 1958 MV reversed its decision and unleashed a full-blooded assault on road racing in all categories.

Private owners were left with the option of riding Manx Nortons and Matchless G50s in their pursuit of John Surtees and others on the all-conquering MVs over the ensuing seasons. The period between 1958 and 1961 was dominated by Surtees, an era where he won 5 TT Races and an incredible six world championships.

During 1958 and 1959 Bob continued to ride the Manx Norton and 7R AJS at the Island and in mainland English meetings. At the 1959 TT he finished fifth in the rain-lashed Senior and won the 500cc Formula 1 event, held during TT week.

This was a one-off experiment, eligible only to private entrants and barring works machinery. Bob's great friend, Alastair King won the 350 Formula 1 race on an AJS; and at the time it was warmly remembered as a dose of 'Double Scotch'.

In 1960 Bob received an approach from Honda to ride their machines in the forthcoming season; however he objected to their regimen, as to where he could or could not enter. They came back in 1961 with a more flexible arrangement, where he could still ride the Potts' Nortons.

At the 1961 Lightweight TT, Bob made a meteoric start, raising the lap record to 99.58 mph, only to have the Honda seize up on him, due to a major oil leak. His Senior TT was more rewarding, with a hard-fought second place behind Mike Hailwood's Norton. In third place was Aussie Tom Phillis on a prototype Norton 'Domiracer', a race version of the model 88 roadster.

The Ulster Grand Prix was generally a happy hunting ground for Bob Mac, where he won the

1961 250 Lightweight race on the Honda. At the 1962 Lightweight TT he raised the lap record to 99.61 mph, only to retire with electrical problems.

He also rode in Grand Prix events with Honda and Bianchi, with podium finishes in Holland, Belgium and East Germany; while still competing in non-championship meetings, and one such event was at Oulton Park, Cheshire in August 1962.

After a bad start in the Senior final, which was run in appalling weather conditions he battled his way to the lead, only to crash and sustain serious head injuries. After nine days in hospital, he died, an outstanding racer and personality, whom Geoff Duke named as, 'the finest rider in the world'.

Author's Tribute

Summarizing those immediate post-war winners, the Manx Grand Prix opened the door to works status to a host of talented riders. Among those deserving particular mention are Ernie Lyons and Ken Bills, both of whom became members of the 1947 Norton works team. Dickie Dale achieved fame, mainly with Italian teams, plus occasional appearances on works Nortons.

Surely the greatest of those Manx winners was Geoff Duke, gaining three World Championships with Norton, and his move to Gilera in 1953 resulting in a further three titles; 1953-1954-1955. Dave Bennett, Senior winner in 1951 seemed poised for greatness as a Norton works rider, only to lose his life in tragic circumstances at the 1952 Swiss Grand Prix.

The late, great Bob McIntyre is best remembered for his 1957 double at the Golden Jubilee TT. He was also a strong contender for the 500cc world championship that same year, only to be cruelly thwarted with physical problems at the final event at Monza. Throughout his career Bob battled mightily against adversity and ill-fortune, and his fatal accident at Oulton Park in August 1962 was keenly felt by his host of fans and fellow riders alike.

There are few sporting activities to match motorcycle road racing at its highest level, both in spectacle and its undeniable element of danger. With our focus on the Isle of Man there is no easy way of sidestepping its alarming casualty list, from Victor Surridge of 1911 to the present day. Admittedly its surface and conditions have progressed from a pot-holed indifferent track to that of billiard-table smoothness by comparison.

However lap speeds have advanced to incredible figures, averaging around the 130 mph region; posing the question; do today's riders face a greater challenge than those veterans of pre-Kaiser war days? There can be no reliable answer to such a situation; comparing current champions with those pioneering titans. In their hey-day every champion was equal to the very best of his contemporaries, so let them be remembered as the greatest of the greats of their particular era.

Author profile

Australian author Murray McLeod is also an accredited artist/illustrator with several publications to his name. These are focused on aviation history, plus two motorcycle titles; 'TT Legends' and the 'Unapproachable Norton', covering that same exciting period of road racing from the 1920's to the 1960's.

Another of his publications, and one that covers a vastly different arena is 'Aussie Tennis Legends'; an appreciation of the esteem in which Australia was held over many years of international and Davis Cup participation.

Email: mcleodart@westnet.com.au

http://www.mcleodart.com.au

Printed in Great Britain
by Amazon